D0396562

A New Leash on Life

rachaelhale

HARVEST HOUSE PUBLISHERS

EUGENE, OREGON

A New Leash on Life

Text copyright © 2008 by Harvest House Publishers
Published by Harvest House Publishers
Eugene, Oregon 97402

ISBN 13: 978-0-7369-2201-2
ISBN 10: 0-7369-2201-6

www.rachaelhale.com

Design and production by Garborg Design Works, Savage, Minnesota

Harvest House Publishers has made every effort to trace the ownership of all poems
and quotes. In the event of a question arising from the use of a poem or quote, we
regret any error made and will be pleased to make the necessary correction in future
editions of this book.

Verses are taken from the HOLY BIBLE, NEW INTERNATIONAL VERSION®. NIV®.
Copyright©1973, 1978, 1984 by the International Bible Society. Used by permission of
Zondervan. All rights reserved.

Printed in China

08 09 10 11 12 13 14 15 / LP / 10 9 8 7 6 5 4 3 2 1

Become a possibilitarian. No matter how dark things seem to be or actually are, raise your sights and see the possibilities—always see them, for they're always there.

NORMAN VINCENT PEALE

Be happy. It is a way of being wise.

SIDONIE-GABRIELLE COLETTE

be happy

One of the things I learned the
hard way was it does not pay to
get discouraged. Keeping busy
and making optimism a way of life
can restore your faith in yourself.

LUCILLE BALL

To be alive, to be able to see, to walk...it's all a miracle. I have adapted the technique of living life from miracle to miracle.

ARTHUR RUBINSTEIN

imagination

Imagination is more important than knowledge.

ALBERT EINSTEIN

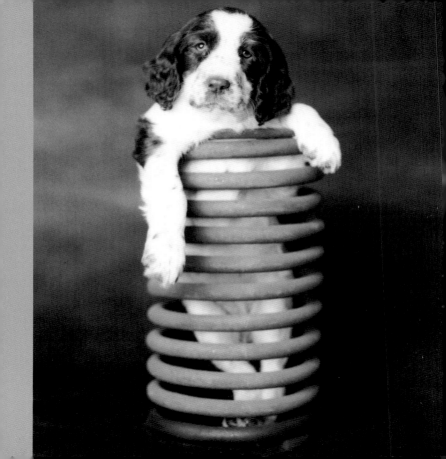

The greatest discovery of any generation is that human beings can alter their lives by altering the attitudes of their minds.

ALBERT SCHWEITZER

attitude

Happiness isn't about what happens to us—it's about how we perceive what happens to us. It's the knack of finding a positive for every negative, and viewing a setback as a challenge. If we can just stop wishing for what we don't have, and start enjoying what we do have, our lives can be richer; more fulfilled— and happier. The time to be happy is now.

LYNN PETERS

character

It is our attitude at the beginning of a difficult undertaking which, more than anything else, will determine its outcome.

WILLIAM JAMES

Character is power.

BOOKER T. WASHINGTON

Far away there in the sunshine are my highest aspirations. I may not reach them, but I can look up and see their beauty, believe in them, and try to follow where they lead.

LOUISA MAY ALCOTT

aspiration

The ultimate measure of a man is not where he stands in moments of comfort, but where he stands at times of challenge and controversy.

MARTIN LUTHER KING JR.

friendship

By friendship you mean the greatest love, the greatest usefulness, the most open communication, the noblest sufferings, the severest truth, the heartiest counsel, and the greatest union of minds of which brave men and women are capable.

JEREMY TAYLOR

15

A loyal friend laughs at your jokes when they're not so good, and sympathizes with your problems when they're not so bad.

ARNOLD H. GLASOW

Blessed are they who have the gift of making friends, for it is one of God's best gifts. It involves many things, but above all, the power of going out of one's self, and appreciating whatever is noble and loving in another.

THOMAS HUGHES

The only service a friend can really render is to keep up your courage by holding up to you a mirror in which you can see a noble image of yourself.

GEORGE BERNARD SHAW

Whatever is true, whatever is noble, whatever is right, whatever is pure, whatever is lovely, whatever is admirable—if anything is excellent or praiseworthy—think about such things.... And the God of peace will be with you.

THE BOOK OF PHILIPPIANS

Of all the heavenly gifts that mortal men commend,
What trusty treasure in the world can countervail a friend?

NICHOLAS GRIMALD

trusty

A true friend is
the gift of God,
and He only who
made hearts can
unite them.

ROBERT SOUTH

Friendship without
self-interest is
one of the rare
and beautiful
things of life.

JAMES F. BYRNES

courage

You gain strength, courage, and confidence
by each experience in which you really stop
to look fear in the face. You are able to say to
yourself, "I have lived through this horror. I can
take the next thing that comes along."

ELEANOR ROOSEVELT

Your worst days are never so bad that you are beyond the reach of God's grace. And your best days are never so good that you are beyond the need of God's grace.

JERRY BRIDGES

grace

When you get into a tight place where you feel you can't go on, hold on, for that is just the place and the time that the tide will turn.

HARRIET BEECHER STOWE

When one door of happiness closes, another opens; but often we look so long at the closed door that we do not see the one which has opened for us.

HELEN KELLER

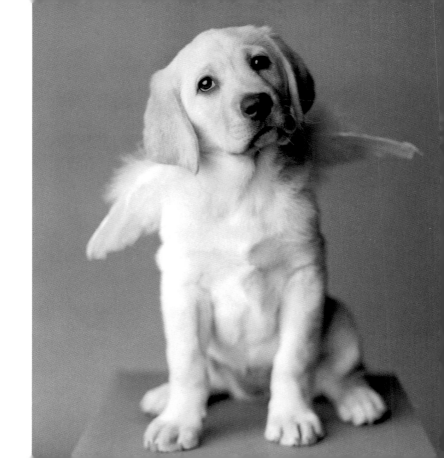

God stirs up our comfortable nests, and pushes us over the edge of them, and we are forced to use our wings to save ourselves from fatal falling. Read your trials in this light, and see if your wings are being developed.

HANNAH WHITALL SMITH

trials

When it is dark enough, you can see the stars.

CHARLES A. BEARD

Good timber does not grow with ease;
the stronger the wind, the stronger the trees.

J. WILLARD MARRIOTT

persist

I will persist until I succeed. Always will
I take another step. If that is of no avail
I will take another, and yet another.
In truth, one step at a time is not too
difficult...I know that small attempts,
repeated, will complete any undertaking.

OG MANDINO

We need time
to dream, time
to remember,
and time to
reach the infinite.
Time to be.

GLADYS TABER

May each day unfold for you like roses,
sparkling in the dew,
that open to the morning sun and bloom
until the day is through.
And may each passing moment bring a song
as pure as angels sing,
but may there be above all things a peace
that only God can bring.

AUTHOR UNKNOWN

Enjoy the successes that you have, and don't be too hard on yourself when you don't do well. Too many times we beat up on ourselves. Just relax and enjoy it.

PATTY SHEEHAN

relax

Happiness is the art of relaxation.

MAXWELL MALTZ

He enjoys true leisure who has
time to improve his soul's estate.

HENRY DAVID THOREAU

leisure

To be able to fill leisure intelligently is the
last product of civilization, and at present
very few people have reached this level.

BERTRAND RUSSELL

life

How far you go in life depends on you being
tender with the young, compassionate with
the aged, sympathetic with the striving, and
tolerant of the weak and the strong. Because
someday in life you will have been all of these.

GEORGE WASHINGTON CARVER

Live your life while
you have it. Life is a
splendid gift—there is
nothing small about it.

FLORENCE NIGHTINGALE

Be glad of life because it gives you the chance to
love, to work, to play, and to look up at the stars.

HENRY VAN DYKE

Experience is not what happens to you. It is what you do with what happens to you.

Reflect upon your present blessings, of which every man has many; not on your past misfortunes, of which all men have some.

experience

40

Only those
who dare to fail
greatly can ever
achieve greatly.

ROBERT F. KENNEDY

achieve

Life is no brief candle to me. It is sort of a splendid
torch which I have got hold of for a moment,
and I want to make it burn as brightly as possible
before handing it on to future generations.

GEORGE BERNARD SHAW

The future belongs to those who
believe in the beauty of their dreams.

ELEANOR ROOSEVELT

inspiration

We get new ideas from
God every hour of our
day when we put our trust
in Him—but we have to
follow that inspiration up
with perspiration—we have
to work to prove our faith.
Remember that the bee
that hangs around the hive
never gets any honey.

ALBERT E. CLIFFE

You will find as you look back upon your life that the moments when you have really lived are the moments when you have done things in the spirit of love.

HENRY DRUMMOND

Love is a fruit in season at all times, and within the reach of every hand.

MOTHER TERESA

Love is a great
beautifier.

LOUISA MAY ALCOTT

Beautiful

If I planted a flower every time I thought of you,
I could walk in my garden forever.

AUTHOR UNKNOWN

For a small child there is no division between playing and learning; between the things he or she does "just for fun" and things that are "educational." The child learns while living and any part of living that is enjoyable is also play.

PENELOPE LEACH

To live exhilaratingly in and for the moment is deadly
serious work, fun of the most exhausting sort.

BARBARA GRIZZUTI HARRISON

It is a happy talent to
know how to play.

RALPH WALDO EMERSON

fun

We don't stop playing
because we turn old,
but turn old because
we stop playing.

AUTHOR UNKNOWN

We may run, walk, stumble, drive, or fly, but let us never lose sight of the reason for the journey, or miss a chance to see a rainbow on the way.

GLORIA GAITHER

chances

Keep on going and the chances are that you will stumble on something, perhaps when you are least expecting it. I have never heard of anyone stumbling on something sitting down.

CHARLES F. KETTERING

Become an answer to someone else's prayer. Visit a sick relative or friend, call someone and encourage them, mow a neighbor's yard, give your spouse a back rub, write a check for a local charity, compliment a coworker, volunteer at a shelter for the homeless. Lift your spirits by lifting someone else's load.

TRACY MULLINS AND ANN SPANGLER

God doesn't send them because we deserve it. He sends them because we need help. Angels are literally messengers of God's mercy.

MAC HAMMOND

What lies behind us and what lies before us are tiny matters compared to what lies within us.

RALPH WALDO EMERSON

faith

Consider it pure joy…whenever you face trials of many kinds, because you know that the testing of your faith develops perseverance.

THE BOOK OF JAMES

I try to avoid looking forward or backward,
and try to keep looking upward.

CHARLOTTE BRONTE

lessons

The difficulties we experience always
illuminate the lessons we need most.

AUTHOR UNKNOWN

That's what it takes to be a hero,
a little gem of innocence inside
you that makes you want to
believe that there still exists a
right and wrong, that decency
will somehow triumph in the end.

LISE HAND

innocence

Life at its best is a series of challenges. A big
enough challenge will bring out strengths and
abilities you never knew you had. Take on your
challenges and you will bring yourself to life.

AUTHOR UNKNOWN

Don't go through life,
grow through life.

ERIC BUTTERWORTH